MILITARY MACHINES

TANKS

BY CHARLES MARLIN

WWW.APEXEDITIONS.COM

Copyright © 2025 by Apex Editions, Mendota Heights, MN 55120. All rights reserved. No part of this book may be reproduced or utilized in any form or by any means without written permission from the publisher.

Apex is distributed by North Star Editions:
sales@northstareditions.com | 888-417-0195

Produced for Apex by Red Line Editorial.

Photographs ©: Shutterstock Images, cover, 13, 16–17, 20–21, 24; Corbis Historical/Getty Images, 1, 14–15; Cpl. Nicole A. LaVine/US Marine Corps, 4–5; Capt. Evan Cain/DVIDS, 6–7; Sgt. Chad Menegay/US Army/DVIDS, 8–9; Jack Sullivan/Alamy, 10–11; Hulton-Deutsch/Corbis Historical/Getty Images, 12; Spc. LaTasha Ross/US Army National Guard/DVIDS, 18; Staff Sgt. Austin Berner/US Army Reserve/DVIDS, 19, 29; Pfc. Jaimee Perez/US Army/DVIDS, 22–23; Lance Cpl. Israel Chincio/US Marine Corps, 25; Cpl. William J. Jackson/USMC/DVIDS, 26–27

Library of Congress Control Number: 2024913140

ISBN
979-8-89250-341-9 (hardcover)
979-8-89250-379-2 (paperback)
979-8-89250-451-5 (ebook pdf)
979-8-89250-417-1 (hosted ebook)

Printed in the United States of America
Mankato, MN
012025

NOTE TO PARENTS AND EDUCATORS

Apex books are designed to build literacy skills in striving readers. Exciting, high-interest content attracts and holds readers' attention. The text is carefully leveled to allow students to achieve success quickly. Additional features, such as bolded glossary words for difficult terms, help build comprehension.

TABLE OF CONTENTS

CHAPTER 1
SOLDIER SUPPORT 4

CHAPTER 2
TANK HISTORY 10

CHAPTER 3
WEAPONS AND ARMOR 16

CHAPTER 4
TEAM EFFORT 22

COMPREHENSION QUESTIONS • 28
GLOSSARY • 30
TO LEARN MORE • 31
ABOUT THE AUTHOR • 31
INDEX • 32

CHAPTER 1

SOLDIER SUPPORT

A group of soldiers attack a base. But enemy fire pushes them back. The soldiers hide behind cover. Soon, a tank rolls past. It heads for the enemy.

During battles, soldiers in tanks may work together with soldiers on foot.

Enemy soldiers fire on the tank. But the tank's **armor** stops their bullets. Next, the enemies fire a powerful **missile**. The tank shoots it out of the air.

M1 Abrams tanks can shoot targets from nearly 2.5 miles (4 km) away.

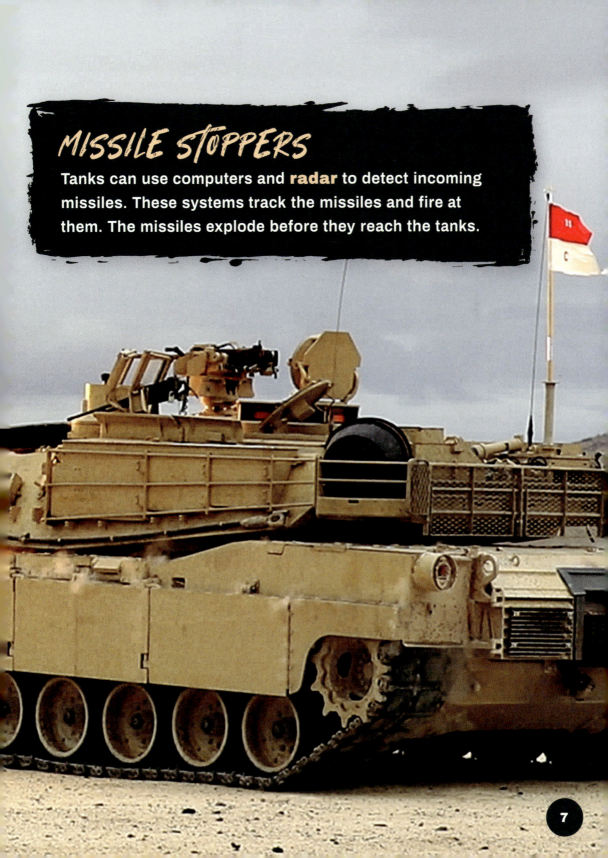

MISSILE STOPPERS

Tanks can use computers and **radar** to detect incoming missiles. These systems track the missiles and fire at them. The missiles explode before they reach the tanks.

An M1 Abrams tank can travel more than 300 miles (480 km) before refueling.

The tank pushes forward. The enemy has to fall back. The attacking soldiers leave their cover. They run into the base.

FAST FACT

Most tanks can move 30 to 40 miles per hour (48 to 64 km/h).

CHAPTER 2

Tank History

Tanks came from armored cars. These cars became common in the early 1900s. They had both armor and **weapons**. Many used steam engines.

The Rolls-Royce Mk1 was an armored car built in 1914. Militaries used it in several wars.

Tracks helped tanks cross over trenches or holes in the ground.

Many militaries built tanks during World War I (1914–1918). The tanks used tracks instead of wheels. The tracks helped tanks move over rough ground.

TRENCH WARFARE

Many World War I battles took place near **trenches**. Barbed wire, machine guns, and **artillery** stopped soldiers from crossing battlefields. Tanks could break through those defenses.

During World War I, soldiers set up barbed wire to slow down enemies.

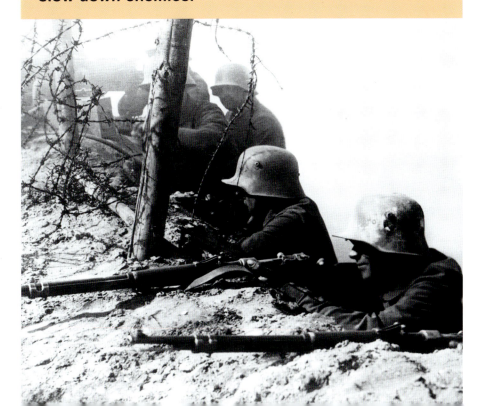

Tanks became even more common during World War II (1939–1945). They got stronger armor and more powerful weapons. Better engines also helped them move faster.

FAST FACT

In 2024, Russia had more than 12,000 tanks. That was the most of any country.

The United States built more than 50,000 Sherman tanks during World War II.

CHAPTER 3

WEAPONS AND ARMOR

At first, some tanks were light and fast. Others had thick armor and strong weapons. Today, most tanks combine speed, thick armor, and strong weapons.

Modern tanks typically have one large gun and a few smaller guns.

Some turrets can spin all the way around in a few seconds.

A tank's main gun sits on the turret. The gun can shoot many types of **ammunition**. Some types damage other tanks. Others target aircraft or soldiers.

AMMUNITION

Tanks fire powerful rounds. HEAT rounds explode when they hit a target. Sabot rounds pierce another tank's armor. Then they shoot out hot metal. The metal burns everything inside the tank.

Sabot rounds have sharp ends that can punch through thick armor.

Tank armor has several layers. Some layers use metal plates. Others are made from ceramic. This material is tough but light. The layers help keep the tank's crew safe.

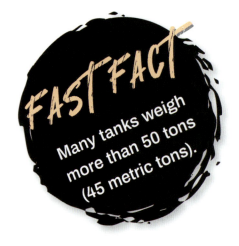

FAST FACT
Many tanks weigh more than 50 tons (45 metric tons).

Some tanks use light armor. That way, they can move quickly.

CHAPTER 4

TEAM EFFORT

Tank crews usually include four soldiers. A driver steers the tank. A gunner aims and fires the main gun. A loader places rounds into the gun. And a commander leads the crew.

Most crew members sit inside the turret.

Drivers sit in the front. They use **periscopes** to see outside. Drivers may use wheels, levers, or handlebars to steer.

Periscopes sit above drivers. Drivers can see outside while staying safe in the tank.

Tanks have many controls for firing and steering.

FAST FACT

Some early tanks stopped moving to shoot. Today, sensors help tanks aim while moving.

SMALL SPACES

Tanks have trouble moving in small spaces. So, narrow city streets can be risky. Tanks may not be able to move to safety. They may not see enemies.

Tank crews may train alongside soldiers on foot. They learn how to fight side by side.

Tanks often work alongside other troops. For example, tanks can clear mines from battlefields for soldiers. And large airplanes can carry tanks to faraway battles.

COMPREHENSION QUESTIONS

Write your answers on a separate piece of paper.

1. Write a few sentences describing the main ideas of Chapter 2.

2. Which fact about tanks is most interesting to you? Why?

3. Which member of a tank crew fires the main gun?
    A. the driver
    B. the loader
    C. the gunner

4. How does being able to shoot many types of ammunition help tanks?
    A. Some types of ammunition act as armor.
    B. Crews do not have to aim when firing some types.
    C. Crews can pick the best type for each target.

5. What does **defenses** mean in this book?

*Barbed wire, machine guns, and artillery stopped soldiers from crossing battlefields. Tanks could break through those **defenses**.*

- **A.** places with few soldiers
- **B.** things that stop attackers
- **C.** ways of moving through an area

6. What does **risky** mean in this book?

*Tanks have trouble moving in small spaces. So, narrow city streets can be **risky**. Tanks may not be able to move to safety.*

- **A.** safe
- **B.** unsafe
- **C.** easy

Answer key on page 32.

GLOSSARY

ammunition

Objects that are shot from weapons.

armor

Coverings that keep people or things safe.

artillery

Large guns, often mounted on wheels.

missile

An object that is shot or launched as a weapon.

periscopes

Tube-shaped tools that use mirrors to help people see things that would be blocked otherwise.

radar

A system that sends out radio waves to locate objects.

trenches

Long, narrow ditches dug into the ground.

weapons

Things that are used to cause harm.

TO LEARN MORE

BOOKS

Banks, Anita. *US Army*. Mendota Heights, MN: Apex Editions, 2023.

Hustad, Douglas. *US Army Equipment and Vehicles*. Minneapolis: Abdo Publishing, 2022.

Schuh, Mari. *Tanks and Other Military Vehicles.* North Mankato, MN: Capstone Publishing, 2023.

ONLINE RESOURCES

Visit **www.apexeditions.com** to find links and resources related to this title.

ABOUT THE AUTHOR

Charles Marlin is an author, editor, and avid cyclist. He lives in rural Iowa.

INDEX

A
armor, 6, 10, 14, 16, 19–20
armored cars, 10

C
crews, 20, 22

E
engines, 10, 14

H
HEAT rounds, 19

M
missiles, 6–7

P
periscopes, 24

R
radar, 7

S
sabot rounds, 19

T
tracks, 12
trenches, 13
troops, 27
turret, 18

W
weapons, 10, 14, 16
World War I, 12–13
World War II, 14

ANSWER KEY:
1. Answers will vary; 2. Answers will vary; 3. C; 4. C; 5. B; 6. B